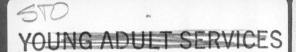

FOREST RESOURCES

FOREST RESOURCES

JANE B. WHIPPLE

FRANKLIN WATTS
NEW YORK | LONDON | TORONTO | SYDNEY | 1985
A FIRST BOOK

Map by Vantage Art, Inc.

Photographs courtesy of:
The Bettmann Archive: p. 5;
U.S. Forest Service: pp. 16, 20, 21, 36, 39;
International Paper Company: pp. 24, 39, 40, 48, 50, 52;
AP/Wide World Photos: p. 32.

Library of Congress Cataloging in Publication Data

Whipple, Jane B.
Forest resources.

(A First book)
Bibliography: p.
Includes index.
Summary: Examines America's forests and their use,
describing the history of forest use and protection, the
national forests, fire and other major threats, and the
resources provided by forests.
1. Forests and forestry—Juvenile literature.
2. Forest products—Juvenile literature. [1. Forests
and forestry] I. Title.
SD376.W48 1985   333.75'0973   84-20939
ISBN 0-531-04909-4

CONTENTS

2274252

FOR A.B.C., WHO
COLLECTS DRIFTWOOD
AND KEEPS
THE FIRES BURNING

FOREWORD

THE HIDDEN FOREST

Strange as it may seem, even though you may be sitting in a modern steel-and-concrete building as you read this, you are actually in the middle of a hidden forest. Wood and other forest products are all around you, close enough to touch.

Your pencil is made of wood from the "pencil cedar" tree.

Your paper lunch bag is made from the loblolly pines of Georgia.

The table or desk next to you may be made of oak or fir plywood. Even if the furniture is plastic, it contains cellulose from spruce, western hemlock, or Monterey pine.

Your baseball bat is made of ash.

The piano nearby may have a mahogany or rosewood case. Inside, its sounding board is made of spruce.

The shirt on your back is probably made of synthetics that originally came from the forest.

Even the page you're reading comes from a tree—the hidden forest that is everywhere around us and on which we all depend.

This book is about forests and about how we have used (and sometimes abused) them. It is the account of a narrow escape. Only a century ago, our forests were disappearing. We were using them up faster than they could grow. It is the story of how a bad case of asthma helped save them—when an ailing president-to-be, young Theodore Roosevelt, became a nature lover. It is the story of the many hazards that still face our forests, and of the ways modern-day experts fight back, using fires to put out fires, and insects to attack other pests.

Most of all, it is the story of the green wonder of the forests that cover, beautify, and regularly color the land, of their many and surprising uses, and of the importance of handling them with care so that they may continue to renew themselves for the delight and use of future generations.

CHAPTER ONE

SETTLERS AND LUMBERJACKS

When the first colonists arrived in the New World more than three centuries ago, they found a land where forests came right down to the edge of the sea. The huge stands of timber were a source of wonder and amazement to these people from the British Isles and western Europe. Most forests in the Old World had been destroyed long before America was discovered.

The Pilgrims who sailed into Provincetown harbor in 1620 marveled at "so goodly a land, and wooded to the brink of the seas . . . with oaks, pines, juniper, sassafras, and other sweet-wood." In America, they had found a land of great beauty and one where firewood, fencing, and lumber were free for the taking. Like the forests, the supply of wood seemed endless. A favorite tall tale told by the colonists was that a squirrel could travel from the Atlantic coast to the banks of the Mississippi River without once coming down out of the trees.

But the towering forests inspired more than thankfulness and awe—they also inspired fear. The dense stands of trees were seen as an obstacle, even as a menace. The deep woods hid native warriors who were sometimes hostile. They were inhabited by many wild animals. And, as a practical matter, trees covered land needed for farming. The settlers' first task was to raise foodcrops, otherwise they could not survive. And so began the backbreaking work of destroying the forest to make farmland.

One of the best accounts of how the land was cleared was given by a French visitor, the Marquis de Chastellux. His diary, written in 1780 during a journey through Connecticut, gives this account of the work of an early settler: "He begins by felling all the smaller trees and some strong branches of the large ones; these he makes use of as fences to the first field he wishes to clear. He next boldly attacks those immense oaks or pines, which one would take for the ancient lords of the territory he is usurping; he strips them of their bark, or lays them open all around with his ax." With their bark destroyed, the large trees died; the following spring they were skeletons without leaves, and eventually the settler got rid of them by burning them to the ground. Meanwhile, the Marquis reported, "The grass grows rapidly. There is pasturage for the cattle the very first year. . . . The next year the same course is repeated, when, at the end of two years, the planter has wherewithal to subsist and even to send some articles to market."

The homesteaders made steady inroads in the forest. By 1804, there was a shortage of wood in Massachusetts. In Connecticut, nearly three-quarters of the land was eventually cleared for farming—it turned out to be poor, rocky land, and many farms were later abandoned. The woods crept back. But they were not like the unbroken forests with towering white pines that had greeted the early settlers.

The axes of the farmers were soon followed by those of the loggers. In fact, lumber was this country's first industry. There was a sawmill at Jamestown, Virginia, as early as 1622; twelve years later, a second mill was built on the coast of Maine.

The fine timbers of the New World were desperately needed by the Old World, which had nearly run out of wood. In the early

Early settlers cleared the land and used
the trees they felled to build their log cabins.

years of the colony, the finest trees of all, New England's white pines, were reserved for the British Royal Navy. The tallest and straightest of these towering trees were branded with the mark of a broad arrow, which meant that they were to be saved for the king. White pine trunks made perfect masts for Britain's wooden warships. Yokes of oxen hauled them out of the forest and down to the wharves. There they were loaded aboard ships for transport to England. The ships had been built just for this purpose, with long, flat decks. Each of them could hold at least fifty masts.

The wood of other trees was also in demand, by American as well as British shipbuilders. Red cedar and locust from the Chesapeake Bay area of Virginia and Maryland were used to build naval and merchant ships. Pitch pine from Georgia and the Carolinas was used for decking. In the days when the great clipper ships were being built in the East Coast ports, the strong, heavy wood of the live oak was highly prized. The live oak grows along the Southern Coast, especially in the swamps of Florida and Georgia. It is a gnarled, twisted tree with an enormous spread to its branches—sometimes as much as 168 feet (51 m). Live oak was dragged out of the swamps and sent north on coastal schooners. It was twice as expensive as other woods, but shipwrights still demanded it because it was strong enough to withstand the steady pounding of heavy seas for many years.

The settlers needed wood for many things other than boatbuilding. Wood was also used for houses, furniture, wagons, barrels, fence posts, and fuel. The loggers had to hustle to keep up with the demand.

In the early days when the forests seemed endless, loggers cut down the finest trees in an area and then moved on. This was known as "cut-out-and-get-out" logging. A few farsighted people did object. William Penn, the founder of Pennsylvania, required that settlers keep one acre of forest for every five acres of land they cleared. But he was unusual. Most colonists considered the forests a nuisance to be cleared and burned so that they could get on with their farming.

After New England and the East Coast had been stripped of the best wood, loggers followed the settlers across the country. By 1875, Michigan, Minnesota, and Wisconsin were the states producing the largest quantities of lumber. Eventually the forests there had been logged bare, and the center of the logging industry moved to the Northwest.

As the lumbermen moved west, they found bigger timber and more rugged forests. The job of getting lumber to the mills became more difficult, and new ways of moving the huge logs had to be found. Four to six spans of oxen were hitched to the logs, and the huge, lumbering beasts then dragged them through the woods. Because the forest floor was apt to be damp and muddy, special roads were built. After the largest trees had been felled, all the saplings along both sides of a passageway were cut down. The saplings, sheared of their branches, were laid side by side across the path, forming the base of a road. It was called a *skid road* because the logs were skidded over it.

Rivers had been used since the earliest days to carry lumber downstream to the mills. The loggers continued to use them whenever they were nearby. When the ice broke up in the spring, huge *log booms*—rafts made up of thousands of tree trunks— started on their way to the mills. They were herded by boom men, who rode the logs and steered them by using long pike polls and shorter pointed polls called *peaveys.*

But much of the Northwest forest grew in areas with deep ravines and steep slopes, where there were not always convenient rivers at hand. So the loggers built wooden *chutes,* or slides, down which the logs thundered. The chutes rested on wooden trestles arching high over the ravines. They curved and twisted down the mountainsides like toboggan runs. *Lumberjacks* sometimes risked their lives by riding the trunks of the forest giants as they hurtled down the slopes, picking up speed as they went.

Sometimes *flumes,* wooden troughs that could be filled with water, were used to carry logs from one lake to another. A lake high on a mountainside would be dammed, and a wooden flume was built leading down to a lower lake or pond. When the level of the lakes rose in the spring, the dam was opened, spilling water and logs into the flume and down to the lower body of water. This was a good way to move logs nearer the foot of the mountain. There they could be floated downstream (if there were a river nearby) or loaded on wagons bound for the sawmill.

The life of the lumberjacks was rough and dangerous. Most of them were young—and all of them were strong and daring. For the most part, they were men without families or homes. When a job was finished, they moved on to the next logging camp. Lumberjacks worked for long hours in all kinds of weather and under extremely dangerous conditions. They were used to seeing their buddies crushed by rolling logs or falling trees. When payday came, they left the woods for the nearest town and spent their pay in bars and honkytonks. The seedy, run-down sections of towns are still called "skid roads," or "skid rows," after the rough roads the loggers built in the woods.

Trees were felled with crude tools—axes and huge crosscut saws known as *misery whips.* The lumberjacks who felled the trees stood on wooden springboards, slabs of wood notched into the tree trunks. They made their first cuts high above the ground where the trunks narrowed, leaving tall stumps behind. Portland, Oregon, like many other western towns, was built in a logged-over area where loggers had cut down the trees but left the stumps standing. It was originally known as Stump Town.

Loggers called their oxen *bulls,* and their nickname for the men who drove them was *bull-whackers.* The skid roads were kept oiled and slick so that the logs would slide easily. Men known as *greasers* ran just behind the bulls, daubing the skid-road with smelly dogfish oil to make it slippery.

An especially daring and skillful lumberjack might become a *high climber.* His job was to scale the tallest tree in the forest, lopping off branches as he climbed. When he neared the top of the swaying tree, perhaps 100 feet (30 m) above the ground, he sawed off the crown. This was called *topping.* It was a moment of great danger because the high climber might be dashed to the ground along with the falling tree top. After it had been topped, the tree's tall trunk was left standing to be used as a *spar tree.* Lines attached to it with block and tackle were used to hoist logs up and over rocks and other obstacles on the forest floor.

Toward the end of the last century, machinery finally came to the woods. Muscle power of men and beasts was gradually replaced by steam. One of the pioneers was a lumberman named John Dolbeer, who built a crude steam engine that could drag big logs out of the woods faster than the bull-whacker and his oxen could. The *Dolbeer donkey,* as the lumberjacks called it, was soon a familiar sight in the Northwest woods.

Loggers then adopted the railroad locomotive for moving deeper into the forest. Tracks were laid and then abandoned as the camps moved on to new sites. On one occasion, a crew was ordered to tear down a railroad trestle because the camp was about to move on. They finished the job, only to discover that a locomotive had been left on the far side of the trestle. The whole structure had to be rebuilt in order to get the locomotive out.

With railroading, new hazards were introduced in the forests. Many of the "locos" were old machines, likely to throw off sparks or even explode, adding to the already large number of forest fires. The tracks laid were usually single lines, used for travel in both directions. Many fatal accidents occurred when a *pole train,* loaded with heavy logs or poles, sped down a steep grade and encountered a *handcar* around the bend.

Handcars were small, open railroad cars used to carry repair-men (or sometimes the crew boss) from the base camp to the spot where the loggers were at work. It wasn't necessary to use a locomotive since these little cars were hand-propelled. The passengers operated a pumping device that made the car move along the rails.

Early sawmills seem primitive by today's standards. These mills were flimsy wooden structures run by waterpower. The same fast-flowing streams carrying logs also ran the mills. At a slightly later date, steam power was used to operate the circular saws and other machinery.

The sawmills were highly dangerous places to work, where exploding boilers, slipping logs, and wooden splinters flying with enough force to pierce the side of a building (or a person's skull) were commonplace. Sometimes circular saws running at high speed broke loose, threatening the lives of anyone in their path. Poor lighting and the absence of safety rules added to the danger.

Along with finished lumber, each of the early sawmills also produced enormous amounts of woodchips, sawdust, and bark. If not disposed of, this waste would have buried the mill under its own debris. The answer to the problem was *wigwam burners.* These were crude structures shaped like teepees, where the chips and sawdust were burned off. The wigwams operated day and night. Long before anyone called it "smog," the whole Northwest Coast was covered by a pall of wood smoke from the thousands of burners.

In order to provide wood for the growing nation, the loggers stripped large areas of their best timber. And in the process, brush and other inflammable trash were left behind in the *logged-over* areas. The dead tree branches, twigs, and dry leaves littering the ground provided fuel for many forest fires.

Reckless logging and the resulting increase in forest fires changed the character of the forests and damaged the surrounding areas. Some kinds of trees, once cut down, could not reestablish themselves, and the trees that replaced them were not as good a source of timber as those of the earlier forest. In other areas, rich topsoil washed away, and the land began to erode. The banks of streams became so dry that they crumbled, dumping dirt into the rivers and leaving large areas of worn-out land. The baked earth lost its ability to soak up water. When rain fell, it ran off over the surface instead of sinking deep into the ground. The result was disastrous flooding.

By the beginning of this century, more than half of the nation's supply of timber was gone. And most of it had been wasted, either left to rot or thrown on huge bonfires and burned. It was almost too late before Americans finally began to realize that they were throwing away one of their continent's most valuable resources.

CHAPTER TWO

RANGERS TO
THE RESCUE

Forests have always been important as a source of wood, but they are more than that. They are places for hiking, camping out, and mountain climbing; refuges where plant life and wild animals flourish; sources of pure water where rain and snow are held in the ground as in a giant sponge; areas where livestock can graze; possible sources of coal, oil, and minerals; and finally, living systems that affect the environment.

One American convinced of the forests' overall importance was Theodore Roosevelt, who probably did more than any other president of the United States to save the forests. "T.R.," who was born in New York City in 1858, became a woodsman almost by accident. He was, in his own words, "a sickly, delicate boy who suffered much from asthma, and frequently had to be taken away on trips to find a place where I could breathe." He was often sent to the country, where he fell in love with the outdoor life and with nature. Not only did his health improve, but he became a horseman, a hunter, and a western rancher, who saw for himself the damage done by what he called the "timber thieves" who threatened to "skin the land."

When Roosevelt became president in 1901, he appointed a committee to study the nation's forests and other natural resources. The committee's report confirmed what he had suspected: the country's forests were rapidly disappearing. During the next eight years, President Roosevelt acted to slow the damage and to protect the remaining forests. He added more than a million acres to the national forests—land under the management of the federal government. He created the first wildlife refuge in the United States—Pelican Island, a three-acre mangrove islet in Florida's Indian River. He started a fire control program and experimental planting in the national forests. He said that his aim was to protect the land "for the people unborn as well as the people now alive."

In order to protect the forests for future generations, T.R. appointed Gifford Pinchot, the first of many dedicated conservationists, to head the United States Forest Service. Pinchot was America's first trained forester. Until the turn of the century, forestry was an unknown science in the United States, so Pinchot studied in Europe, where schools of forestry had existed for many years.

As head of the Forest Service, Pinchot set up research centers and helped colleges and universities start schools of forestry. The research that Pinchot began is still going on today, and scientists continue to search for new ways of protecting the forests.

Together, Pinchot and Roosevelt drew up guidelines that slowed and finally halted the destruction of the forests. Although the programs they started were sound, so much damage had already been done that the forests continued to decline until about 1930, many years after Roosevelt's death. At the lowest point, there were just 600 million acres (247 million hectares) of forest left. Within a decade, Roosevelt and Pinchot's long-range plan finally took effect, and the forests began to recover.

Today about one-third of the United States is covered by forest. There are nearly 388 million acres (153 million hectares) of "commercial" forest—land capable of producing wood suitable for harvesting. More than half of it is owned by private individuals. A little over one-quarter is publicly owned, either by the federal government or by states and municipalities. And the remaining 14 percent is owned by the forest products industry.

Part of the public lands are called national forests. They are under the management of the federal government. There are 155 national forests located in forty-four states, Puerto Rico, and the Virgin Islands. All together, they add up to 89 million acres (36 million hectares). Small parts of them are set aside as wilderness areas to be protected from any kind of development and "where man himself is a visitor who does not remain."

By law, the remaining national forest land must be used for a number of purposes: wildlife preservation, livestock grazing, mining, recreation, watershed land, and timber production. Employing the national forests to satisfy many different needs is called *multiple use*. And one of the most popular of these uses is recreation.

Americans have always liked to rough it—to get out-of-doors and test themselves against nature. This generation, with its emphasis on physical fitness, is no exception. In our national forests, the number of visitors has increased enormously. Twenty million people visit them each year; some national forest resorts have as many as 20,000 skiers a day. National forests near cities have had to close their gates to visitors when the crowds became too large to handle.

In other areas, there is a possibility that people will love their wilderness to death. Near the top of Mount Washington, New Hampshire, for example, lies a meadow where a rare alpine plant, Robbins cinquefoil, blooms each June. It is an endangered species that grows only in this one area. In 1983, the Forest Service spent $7,000 on a low rock wall to enclose the cinquefoil and protect it from hikers' boots. Too many admirers are threatening this tiny, fragile plant, which has been struggling to survive for tens of thousands of years.

The use of ORVs (off road vehicles), including snowmobiles

and motorcycles, is an even greater threat to wildlife and vegetation. They have become so widespread that they have been banned in some places and are limited to roads and special trails in others.

At Glacier National Park in Montana, a boardwalk has been built over a meadow filled with wildflowers. Otherwise the plants would soon be crushed by motorists who climb out of their cars for a glimpse of wilderness. Tire treads and hikers' boots also bring in seeds from outside, and these alien plants sometimes crowd out the rarer varieties that would normally be found there.

Glacier National Park is a good example of other kinds of threats to national parks. All four of its borders are the scene of intense logging and mining. On the Canadian side, much of the land has been logged bare. The lodgepole pines that once grew there have been cut back right to the border, and by 1985 another 100 million board feet (33.3 million meters) of timber will have been harvested. This seriously reduces the feeding area of the park's wild game animals—deer, elk, and bear. These animals need large ranges for hunting and feeding. A small patch of wilderness cannot feed them, although it may be a good home for smaller creatures such as birds, squirrels, mice, chipmunks, rabbits, and raccoons.

Permits for logging in the national forests are issued by the Forest Service, and in recent years the demand for them has become greater and greater. In a recent two-year period, the Forest Service permitted loggers to cut all the trees on almost one million acres (404,858 hectares) of federal land. Harvesting trees on such a huge scale means building new roads into the forest for logging machines. And, of course, it destroys beautiful scenery and wildlife habitat.

The U.S. Forest Service also issues grazing permits. Ranchers are permitted to use national forest land as range for their livestock. At present, more than a million sheep and cattle graze on about 14 million acres (5.67 million hectares) of national forest

*Sheep graze in White River
National Forest in Colorado.*

land in the West. Permits need to be carefully limited, since over-grazing permanently damages the land. Utah's Manti-La Sal National Forest is one area where damage has occurred. In the 1880s, there were nearly three million sheep in Utah. Ranchers had increased their herds over a number of years when there was more rainfall than usual and plenty of grass for the animals. But by 1890, the rainfall had tapered off, and with it the amount of food. The starving herds of sheep proceeded to destroy the native grasses by eating every green shoot in sight. Once the grass cover was gone, juniper and sagebrush sprouted in some areas; in others, the land washed away, leaving bare slopes and deepened gullies.

Some people think that the most important forest product of all is water. Forests slow down the progress of rain from the clouds to the oceans and act as watersheds. A *watershed* is an area that acts as a natural reservoir, holding reserve supplies of fresh water. And this is exactly what forests do.

When there is a downpour, some rain hits bare ground, where it is quickly carried off by streams or rivers. It eventually reaches the ocean, where it is of little value to human beings. But a forest absorbs the rain and then releases it slowly. When rain falls in the deep woods, it is soaked up by the spongy forest floor. Gradually it trickles down to underground reservoirs. When they have filled and the forest floor is brimming with water, little streams appear and flow off to larger streams and rivers. Falling snow, another source of fresh water, piles up on forest floors, where it is shaded from the sun. There the snow may take weeks or even months to melt and find its way down to the underground reservoirs. In contrast, snow in nonforested areas melts rapidly and sometimes causes flooding. Studies have shown that a forest holds fourteen times as much water as an equal area of open field.

Some of the first protests against cut-out-and-get-out logging were the result of dwindling supplies of fresh water. Ranchers in the western states objected to the work of the loggers because it eroded the soil and destroyed the watershed the forests provided. The streams needed by the ranchers to water their cattle dried up and disappeared, leaving bare gullies behind them.

Another role of the national forests, and especially of the wilderness areas, is to provide a safe place for all kinds of wildlife—plants, animals, insects, birds, and reptiles. Many animals once common in North America now exist only in the deep forests or in zoos. The forests are a home for millions of big game animals. They provide a refuge for fifty-eight rare and endangered wildlife species.

One of the big game animals of the forest is the Roosevelt elk, named for Theodore Roosevelt. In 1900 this species was in danger of extinction. The elk were butchered by hunters, partly for their meat, but especially for their canine teeth. Elk's teeth brought a good price in those days because gentlemen wore them on their watch chains. When wristwatches became popular, the elk won a temporary reprieve. And today they have found a safe home within the Olympic National Park, where a herd of 5,000 Roosevelt elk survives.

There has always been a tug-of-war between people who think one of the many uses of the national forests is more important than the others. Ranchers, for example, want permits to graze their animals on federal lands, while lumberjacks want permits for logging in the same area. Miners want to explore for coal and oil, while nature lovers want wildlife protection. That tug-of-war goes on today, and, in fact, it has heated up since the energy crisis. The increased demand for coal, oil, and natural gas has put new pressure on the national forests. The growing use of forest products has resulted in more and more logging on federal land. Population is increasing, and Americans are using their forests in increasing numbers for recreation.

It is not always possible to satisfy all these demands. Choices will sometimes have to be made among them. In trying to be fair to all the people who want different things from their forests today, it is important to think of tomorrow. Without careful planning, some of the things the forest provides, such as fresh water and a safe home for wildlife, might be lost forever.

CHAPTER THREE

GIANT SEQUOIAS AND MANGROVE SWAMPS

The many forests of the United States belong to six main forest regions. Each region has a character quite its own, determined by its location and climate. The amount of rainfall, the length of the growing season, the type of soil, the temperature, whether the land is flat or hilly or on a high mountain or in a valley—all play a part in the nature of the forest.

Look at the map on page 26 and you will see how the regions spread across North America. The belt stretching along the West Coast is the Pacific Forest, where giant sequoia are found. Eight hundred miles (1,288 km) inland and at a higher altitude is the Rocky Mountain Forest—the home of the bristlecone pine, Earth's oldest living thing. Arching across America from Alaska to New England is the mighty Northern Forest. Just below it lies the Central Forest, which covers most of the eastern half of the United States and spreads all the way to Arkansas and Oklahoma. Extending from southern Virginia down into Florida and west into Texas are the piney woods of the Southern Forest—the center of today's forest products industry. Smallest of the forest

The six main forest
regions are the
(a) Pacific,
(b) Rocky Mountain,
(c) Northern,
(d) Central,
(e) Southern, and
(f) Tropical.

regions is the Tropical Forest, which is found on the tip of Florida and a small coastal area of Texas.

THE PACIFIC FOREST

Most of the trees in this forest region are *conifers*, which means that they bear cones. The huge stands of Douglas fir, western hemlock, and Sitka spruce in the Pacific Forest are unequaled anywhere in the world. Some people call this forest the Big Woods because many of its trees are true giants. In fact, the giant sequoias of California are the largest living things on Earth—bigger by far than the mightiest elephant or the greatest whale.

The giant sequoia grows on the slopes of the Sierra Nevada Mountains at altitudes of 4,500 to 8,000 feet (1,372–2,438 m). It sometimes reaches a height of over 275 feet (84 m) and may have a girth of 35 feet (11 m). The giant sequoia lives for a great many years; some trees still alive and growing today are 3,500 years old.

The coast redwood is even taller than the giant sequoia, though not as massive. One of them is more than 368 feet (112 m) tall—the height of a twenty-story building. The redwood has a slimmer trunk, however, so its total bulk is less than that of the giant sequoia. The redwood thrives near the coast of the Pacific, where the prevailing westerly winds constantly bathe the trees in the moisture they need to grow.

One of the most important trees in the Pacific Forest is the Douglas fir, which accounts for one-quarter of all timber standing in the United States. The principal trees in the Alaskan part of this forest region are the western hemlock and the Sitka spruce.

The Pacific Forest is an important source of timber. One-third of all the lumber used in the United States comes from these woods, and they also supply one-fifth of the nation's *pulpwood*. Pulpwood trees are the source of *wood pulp,* which is used in making paper and rayon.

THE ROCKY MOUNTAIN FOREST

Inland from the Pacific coast lies the Rocky Mountain Forest. It follows the mountain ranges at heights of 5,000 to 11,000 feet (1,524 to 3,353 m) from Oregon to Oklahoma and Texas. The principal trees are pines, Douglas fir, and Engelmann spruce. One-quarter of all the lumber in the United States comes from this region, but trees grow slowly here, partly because this area receives less rain than the Pacific Forest.

This is a spectacular area with snow-covered mountaintops rearing up above the timberline—an imaginary line at a height of 11,000 feet (3.353 m), above which no trees are able to grow. Just below the timberline, on the high slopes, larch and whitebark pine struggle to survive.

On the dry windswept heights of California's White Mountains stand trees that are the world's oldest living things. They are the bristlecone pines. Experts have found that some of them have been alive for 4,500 years. They first sprouted during the years when Egypt's great pyramids were being built, and were already 4,000 years old when Columbus sailed for America.

The age of a felled tree can be determined by counting the annual growth rings in its trunk: each year the tree adds a new outer circle of woody material to its bulk; the summer growth is darker than the rest and forms a distinct ring. After a tree has been felled, it is easy to find out how old it is by counting the rings in a crosscut section of the trunk. These rings also show scars from fire and lightning, and inroads made by insects. They reveal periods when growth was slowed by drought or speeded up when neighboring trees fell and let more sunlight through.

The age and growth rate of a living tree can also be told by taking a core sample. The core is the centermost part of a tree trunk. In order to take a core sample, the forester cuts a sliver from the tree, extending from the outer bark into the very middle. The growth rings on this sample can be counted in order to find how old the tree is.

THE NORTHERN FOREST

This great forest belt, made up largely of coniferous trees, does not pay any attention to national boundaries. The Northern Forest swings from Alaska all the way across Canada, through Minnesota, the Great Lakes area, and New England, with a finger extending down through the Appalachians to the northern border of Georgia. It is sometimes called the boreal forest, after Boreas, the ancient Greeks' name for the north wind; or the taiga, a Russian word for the similar coniferous forest in Eurasia; or simply the North Woods.

The North Woods are dotted with lakes (Minnesota alone claims to have 10,000 of them) and rivers. It is in these woods that the Indians found a remarkable tree—the paper birch. It has soft, white bark that can be peeled from the trunk in large sheets. Using this white birchbark, the Indians perfected a graceful canoe that was ideally suited for travel in the North Woods, since it was light enough to be carried in places where the streams were blocked by rocks or rapids.

Along with conifers, cone-bearing trees, and the paper birch, the Northern Forest has many kinds of *hardwood* trees. Hardwoods are trees that shed their leaves each year, such as yellow birch, beech, walnut, poplar, and oak. There once were large numbers of American chestnut trees in the Appalachian area, but they have since been killed by disease. Some of the dead chestnut trunks are still standing in "ghost" forests.

The Northern Forest is where the logging industry first started in this country. Maine, New York, and Pennsylvania were the first major timber producers, and after their supplies had been largely used up, Michigan, Minnesota, and Wisconsin took the lead.

The age and growth rate of this tree
can be calculated by counting the rings.
How old do you think the tree is?

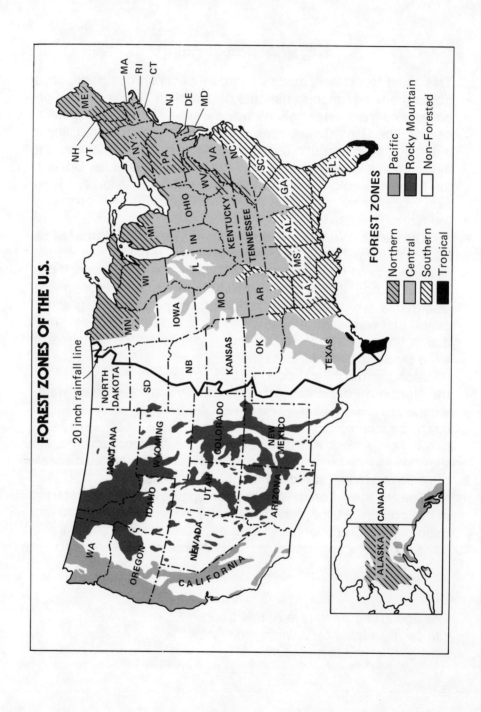

FOREST ZONES OF THE U.S.

20 inch rainfall line

FOREST ZONES

- Northern
- Central
- Southern
- Tropical

- Pacific
- Rocky Mountain
- Non-Forested

MA
RI
CT
NJ
DE
MD
NH
VT
ME
NY
PA
WV
VA
NC
SC
GA
FL
OHIO
KENTUCKY
TENNESSEE
AL
MS
LA
IL
IN
MI
WI
MN
IOWA
MO
AR
KANSAS
OK
TEXAS
NB
SD
NORTH DAKOTA
MONTANA
WYOMING
COLORADO
NEW MEXICO
UTAH
ARIZONA
NEVADA
IDAHO
OREGON
WA
CALIFORNIA

ALASKA
CANADA

THE CENTRAL FOREST

This forest region covers parts of thirty states and ranges all the way from Cape Cod to the Rio Grande and back up to the Canadian border. There are many species of trees in the Central Forest, more than 400 in Illinois alone. Most of them are *deciduous.* They change color in the fall and lose their leaves soon afterward.

The fall colors in New England forests are unequaled anywhere else in the world. In fact, people come here from abroad just to see the sight. At the height of the fall foliage season in New England, all the hotels and inns are full, and sight-seeing buses are a familiar sight on the roads.

The blaze of color is not triggered by frost, as many people believe, but by a reaction of the tree to the short, cool days of autumn. In colder weather, when the days are shorter, the tree stops producing chlorophyll, which makes leaves green, and other colors that have been hidden by the green are then revealed. At the same time, sugar in the leaves turns into a new group of vivid colors—and the result is a glorious display on the mountainsides and in the valleys of the region. The red maple, sugar maple, poplar, beech, and oak are the brightest trees in the fall landscape.

The rich soil that once nourished the woods of this forest in many cases also spelled their doom. Much of the area was cleared for agriculture because it made such fertile farmland. Most of today's forest is relatively new, with only a few pockets remaining of the great forests the early settlers found.

THE SOUTHERN FOREST

The dominant trees of the Southern Forest are the pines—shortleaf, longleaf, slash, and loblolly. In fact, this area is sometimes called the Piney Woods. But there are also some hardwood trees in the region, including maple, oak, elm, and cottonwood.

The Southern Forest lies on the flat, sandy Atlantic Plain, and much of it was cleared in order to grow cotton and tobacco. In Georgia, for example, there were once large stands of oak and hickory, which were cut down to make room for cotton plantations. The soil was impoverished by the crops, and without its forest cover, it soon started to erode. After the land was abandoned as worthless for farming, trees slowly returned. But there are now very few hardwoods. Instead, acre after acre is covered with faster-growing, hardier pines.

A great deal of effort has gone into an attempt to improve lumber and pulpwood production from these woods. Since the region has long summers, mild winters, and plenty of rain, trees grow very quickly here. Today, the Southern Forest produces one-third of all the lumber used in the United States and more than half of the pulpwood.

THE TROPICAL FOREST

At the tip of Florida and in a small part of southeastern Texas is this country's smallest forest region. It is also the least important in terms of forest products. But the trees found in this low-lying, swampy area are unlike any others in the United States.

Among them are the bald cypress, a conifer that sheds its leaves in the fall. It is then very bald indeed. The bald cypress may live for more than 700 years and grow to a height of 100 feet (30 m) or more. During the building boom following World War II, nearly all the bald cypress was cut down. The only large ones remaining are those in protected areas where logging is not permitted.

Smaller varieties of cypress are still found in the Florida Everglades, along with slash pine and, in some remote areas, the royal palm. The royal palm lives up to its name. It is a stately tree with a slender gray-white trunk that rises from the ground for a hundred feet or more before the leaves of the crown branch out against the sky.

Along the coast, there are dense thickets of mangrove trees, which are able to grow in salt water. The mangrove's seeds sometimes drift for hundreds of miles before reaching shallow water where they can root. Mangrove seeds are about the size and shape of cigars; one end is pointed and heavier than the other. When the floating seed grounds on a shallow sand bar, it immediately starts to put out roots from its heavy end, and they pull the little seedling upright. As it grows, other roots arch out from the trunk and the branches, helping to anchor the seedling. These dense roots form a tangled mass that traps debris and silt. In this way, the mangroves actually create islets. The mangrove swamps also help protect the Florida coast from tropical storms. They have often sheltered people, as well. According to some Floridians, the safest place to ride out a hurricane is deep in a swamp on a boat tied snugly to the mangrove roots.

In addition to the six major forest regions of the continental United States are a number of smaller ones. They are Puerto Rico's tropical rain forest; the mesquite forests of the Southwest; the chaparral of the California foothills; the saguaro cactus forest just above the Mexican border; the petrified forest in northern Arizona—a relic of the days of the dinosaur; the rare temperate rain forest of Washington's Olympic Peninsula; and Hawaii's Kauai cloud forest, one of the wettest places on Earth.

Over the last three and a half centuries, this country has changed from a heavily forested land with fewer than a million American Indians living in tribal groups scattered across the wilderness, to a modern industrial society with more than 225 million citizens. It is a wonder that so many vast stands of forest, in their infinite variety, still exist.

CHAPTER FOUR

FIRES AND OTHER DISASTERS

The forests of North America must supply the demands of a growing population and at the same time fight off many hazards. They are attacked by droughts, tree-toppling hurricanes, and fiery lava from volcanoes—as well as by insects and disease, acid rain, and forest fires.

INSECTS AND DISEASE

To the forest, insects are a mixed blessing. They sometimes help and sometimes harm the woods. They serve as food for birds and small mammals, and they help speed up the decay of fallen leaves and tree trunks. But at times, there are too many insects of one kind, and they actually kill the trees.

In a healthy forest, there is a delicate balance. The trees and other plants, the creatures that live in and around them, the humus and soil together with the fungi and other organisms they harbor, the air and water and sunlight, are all in harmony. Any change in the forest may throw it out of balance. If one particular kind of bird disappears, the insects that it fed on may multiply so rapidly that they become a menace. If chemicals are used to destroy an insect pest, they may also kill the natural enemies of another insect and set off a dangerous new population explosion in the forest.

Many insects attack just one species of tree—they may have a taste for spruce buds but not for oak leaves. Such insects cause less damage in wooded areas with many different kinds of trees.

In areas where most of the trees are of the same species, a great many may become infested and die. For example, in the Targhee National Forest of Idaho, 60 percent of the trees are lodgepole pines. The lodgepole pine is straight, tall, and fast-growing. Indians used it to build their lodges (hence its name), and it is now used for fences, log cabins, and telephone poles. The pines in the Targhee forest have been attacked by the mountain pine beetle. Ninety percent of the lodgepoles are dead or dying as the result of an epidemic that started thirty years ago. The forest is now in such bad shape that in order for it to be restored, it will probably be necessary to *clear-cut* the whole area and start over.

Severe damage often occurs when insects or diseases are imported from other countries. Native trees have no defense against a new disease because they have never been exposed to it before. And newly arrived insects may not have any natural enemies in American forests. Partly for this reason, customs inspectors do not allow travelers to bring any fruits or vegetables into the United States. Dutch elm disease, discovered by and named after Dutch scientists, has destroyed millions of elm trees since its arrival here. It is spread by bark beetles. They scurry from one tree to the next, carrying a fungal infection that is lethal to elm trees.

Because insects and disease are so damaging, researchers have found many ways of fighting them and are constantly searching for new methods. The gypsy moth is a good example

of an insect pest that people have tried to eliminate by using various methods.

The first gypsy moths in the United States came here from Europe. A French naturalist, living in Massachusetts, imported them. He was trying to crossbreed gypsy moths with silkworms. In 1869, a few gypsy moth caterpillars escaped from their cage, which had been tipped over during a storm. They were the ancestors of the billions of pests that have eaten the leaves of deciduous trees in the Northeast.

These caterpillars are so greedy that they can devour all the leaves of a good-sized tree overnight. Although they prefer oak trees, they are not fussy eaters. In fact, they will eat nearly any foliage except that of dogwood and mountain laurel. During recent years, they have left millions of acres of leafless trees behind them as they munched their way through the woods.

In an effort to destroy gypsy moths, nearly everything has been tried. At one time, parasites that were natural enemies of the gypsies were imported from Europe and released in the woods. When that didn't solve the problem, a 25-mile-wide (40 km) "barrier zone" was created. This no-man's-land was heavily sprayed with lead arsenate insecticide in an effort to keep the moths from spreading into new territory. But the gypsy moth caterpillars munched on. Even rivers are not enough to halt their slow march through the forests. The caterpillars are able to travel either by crawling on the ground or by swinging from long silken threads that they release from a gland in their heads. In the 1940s, the federal government started spraying infested areas

Gypsy moth damage is clearly visible in
this aerial photograph of rural Pennsylvania.
The trees on the left have been almost
entirely stripped of their foliage while the
trees on the right seemed to be untouched.

from airplanes. The insecticide used was DDT. It killed moths rapidly but also destroyed other wildlife. The next weapon tried was a chemical insecticide, Sevin. Sevin is safer than DDT, but, in addition to moths, it also kills honeybees and "good" insects that are natural enemies of gypsy moths. The latest spray to be tried is Bt, which is made from a bacterium. It does not kill bees but is fatal to all leaf-eating caterpillars—not just those of the gypsy moth.

Another new scheme that has been tried is luring male moths into traps by using a sex scent. The female gypsy moth is unable to fly, so to attract the male, she gives off an odor called a pheromone. Scientists have now managed to make a good imitation of this scent. It works—the males are drawn to the trap—but in heavily infested areas, killing a few males is not nearly enough to stop the invasion.

Experts now feel that the gypsy moth will never be entirely eliminated. Their hope is to lessen the damage done by these hungry caterpillars by seeing to it that there are fewer of them around.

ACID RAIN

Another threat to forests comes from acid rain. Some acid rain is caused by natural occurrences: a volcanic eruption can result in enormous acid clouds which, sooner or later, fall to earth as acid rain or acid snow. It is also caused in modern industrial society by burning fossil fuels—coal, oil, and gas.

The fastest and most dramatic result of acid rain is dead fish. The acid rain poisons lakes and ponds of fresh water, killing all the fish and other animal life and leaving "dead" lakes. There are now 212 "dead" lakes in New York's Adirondack Mountains and 250 others that are in danger.

The threat of acid rain is not limited to the New England states. It has begun to affect other states and large areas in Canada. Damage to forest trees is more gradual than the harm done to the lakes. Trees growing on mountain tops are the first to show signs of damage. Clouds full of acid settle on mountain peaks, subjecting the trees to a poisonous atmosphere. Camels Hump is the third highest peak in the Green Mountains of Vermont. Botanists from the University of Vermont report that the forests of Camels Hump are dying. Another report is from Mount Mitchell, North Carolina: the forest there is dying, too.

FOREST FIRE

The most terrifying of the hazards of the forest is fire. Within a few hours, a major fire can burn thousands of acres, endangering the lives of wild creatures and humans, and causing destruction that will still be evident many years later.

All forest fires are started in one of two ways: by lightning or by human beings. Lightning causes one out of ten fires, but the other nine are started by people—and many of them are lighted deliberately.

Even the Indians used fire to flush out game or to clear brush from their hunting areas, and when the European settlers arrived, fire helped them clear the land for farming. But as settlements spread and logging changed the forests, fire became an even more serious threat. In the old days of cut-out-and-get-out, loggers left behind them in the woods great quantities of *slash*— leafy twigs and branches—as well as dead stumps. When all this debris dried out, it served as tinder for future fires. Disastrous blazes raged out of control over thousands of acres of timberland.

There are several different kinds of fires in forests. One is surface fire, which burns litter and underbrush and often kills saplings. Another is *crown fire,* which blazes from the ground all the way up to the top of a tree, and then advances from treetop to treetop. It is crown fire that is most dreaded, and with good reason. Crown fires burn with such energy that they create their own winds. They may move faster than a person can run. Huge trees

Above: *this is a surface fire in Salmon National Forest, Idaho. The flames in the foreground are from a bed of pine cones. Below: in this crown fire in Boise National Forest, Idaho, the flames have spread from the ground to the top of a tree and are advancing from treetop to treetop.*

literally explode into flames and hurl firebrands—burning cones or branches—which start new fires wherever they land.

The Peshtigo Fire of October 1871 was probably the worst in the history of the United States. No one knows exactly how it started, but it quickly became a roaring inferno because the North Woods were full of tinder-dry slash left behind by the loggers. By the time it ended two days later, 1,638 people had died, and more than a million acres of forest in two states had burned. The mill town of Peshtigo, Wisconsin, was utterly destroyed in the course of an hour. The only people who survived were those who managed to reach the Peshtigo River, where they spent the night dousing their clothing with water, ducking firebrands carried by the wind, and fending off burning logs. In 1894, a forest fire near Hinckley, Minnesota, killed more than 400 people. In 1910, a fire in Idaho, Washington, and Montana burned 3 million acres (1 million hectares), destroying a number of small towns and killing 85 firefighters.

The loggers themselves often started fires accidentally. In tinder-dry forests, the friction caused by dragging logs across the forest floor could ignite the underbrush. Sparks thrown off by crude logging machinery were another source of fire. One of the worst forest fires of modern times was accidentally started by loggers. It was the disastrous Tillamook Burn of August 1933. The Northwest was so dry that summer that the governor of Oregon closed all state forests to logging and asked that loggers on privately owned land also stop work. But some loggers kept on in spite of the warnings. They worked in the early morning hours when there was dew in the air and the moisture somewhat lessened the danger of fire. (This was known as *hoot-owl logging*—working at sunup when owls were about.)

One of the hoot-owl crews, working in Gales Creek Canyon, started to drag a huge Douglas fir log toward the loading area. The friction of the fir's thick bark grinding against the dry forest floor created a spark, which in turn kindled a tiny flame. The fire quickly raged out of control. It created a mushroom cloud that was seen for hundreds of miles. Soot and cinders from the fire blackened the beaches, piling up 2 feet (61 cm) deep on the Oregon coast and falling on ships 500 miles (805 km) at sea. Before the fire ended, it had destroyed 311,000 acres (125,911 ha) of the nation's most beautiful forest land, leaving behind only the smoking stumps of what had been magnificent 400-year-old Douglas firs.

In 1945, the U.S. Forest Service started a national fire prevention program with the now famous Smokey the Bear as its trademark. At first, Smokey was just a drawing on the campaign posters. But in 1950, a real live bear cub, rescued after a fire in New Mexico's Lincoln National Forest, was named Smokey and became the program's mascot. This real Smokey lived at the National Zoo in Washington, D.C., from 1950 until he died in 1976. Now there is a new Smokey, and millions of people go to visit him each year. The Smokey the Bear campaign, with its slogan "only you can prevent forest fires," has succeeded in alerting people to the dangers of carelessness and has probably saved many lives and thousands of acres of woodlands. Still, forest fires continue to burn, and some people continue to light them—on purpose.

Fires started deliberately by arsonists are a major problem in the Southern Forest region. (*Arson* is defined in criminal law as the malicious or spiteful burning of another person's property.) The main cause of fires in the South is arson; and between 1956 and 1981, the number of fires in the area increased from 55,000 to 76,000 a year.

Some arsonists set fires for revenge or out of spite. There have been cases where workers laid off by lumber companies have started fires to "get even." Others were lit by people who felt that the lumber industry had taken over their hunting grounds. And perhaps some vandals start fires just for the thrill of it or because they have had too many drinks.

Many cases of arson are never solved. In November 1980, a Forest Service employee flying in a plane watched as sixteen

*Smokey the Bear at the National Zoo
in Washington, D.C. in 1950*

This bulldozer is being used to dig a ditch that will serve as a fire break to help stop the flames of a forest fire from spreading.

Controlled burning destroys the underbrush that forest fires thrive on.

separate blazes sprang up in the Cohutta Wilderness Area of Georgia. The arsonist, hidden by the forest trees, was never caught. He succeeded in starting the largest forest fire ever to occur in any of the eastern wilderness areas, and the Forest Service spent over $250,000 to fight this one fire.

The United States spends more than $500 million every year in fighting forest fires. The first step is to find them before they have time to spread. Modern technology is used to detect fires at an early stage. At times when there are severe thunderstorms, the skies are constantly scanned by electronic devices that have a range of 250 miles (403 km) and are able to locate thunderbolts strong enough to set trees on fire. Spotter planes are equipped with *infrared sensors*, devices that find *hot spots*—areas where hidden fires may be smoldering. These sensors can also "see" through clouds or smoke. They are able to pinpoint a forest fire even though the visibility may be near zero.

The Forest Service maintains fifty-four *Hot Shot crews,* the elite among firefighters, who are ready to go anywhere at a moment's notice. They are sometimes parachuted into an area near a fire. The *smoke jumpers* then clear spaces where helicopters can unload heavy firefighting equipment, such as water tankers, bulldozers, and fire plows. This equipment is used to cut firebreaks, areas where all the trees and underbrush are cleared in an attempt to halt the spread of the fire. The crews may also start backfires designed to burn *toward* the main blaze and destroy the fuel in the area before the fire front arrives. Planes, air tankers, and helicopters are also used more directly to fight the blaze with chemicals or water.

In recent years, experts have come to feel that not all forest fires are bad. For one thing, the build-up of litter—fuel for future fires—goes on even in forests where there is no logging. Dead leaves, dead trunks, fallen branches, pine cones, and needles— all accumulate on the forest floor. If this debris is allowed to pile up for a period of years, the result may be a very intense crown fire when the woods are finally ignited. Foresters now think that an occasional surface fire may be good for the forest because it removes the tinder that helps a forest burn.

It is also known that some trees, such as the jack pine and the lodgepole pine, need fire. They seed themselves only after fire has swept through the forest. The scales of their seed-bearing cones are held tightly together by sticky resins. These resins melt, releasing the seeds, only at high temperatures. Ponderosa pine seedlings need bare forest soil in order to grow. A forest floor heavily covered with leaves and *mulch* (a protective covering that keeps the soil moist) does not make a good seedbed for them. The seedlings of various other trees need more sunlight than they get in the dense woods and thrive when a fire has created open areas.

One of the best ways of avoiding crown fires is by starving them of fuel. This is exactly what a surface fire does when it burns the litter of the forest floor along with underbrush and grasses. Accordingly, the Forest Service now starts what are called "prescribed burns" in some areas. These prescribed burns are carefully planned in advance. Foresters may bulldoze firebreaks around the area to be burned. Or they may take advantage of such natural firebreaks as lakefronts or riverbanks. The amount of moisture in the air and the direction of the wind are also carefully calculated. And not only does the careful use of the prescribed burns help to prevent uncontrolled crown fires, but it also helps the forest grow by opening up dense woods to sunlight and, in some instances, releasing seeds. That is why foresters now feel that fires, like insects, are a mixed blessing in the forest.

CHAPTER FIVE

FOREST BOUNTY

An even bigger threat to the forests than disease, acid rain, or fire, is the rapidly growing demand for wood and wood products. Trees are useful in so many ways that modern society uses nearly 5,000 products that come from the forest. Trees are used for everything from food wrappers to toilet paper, from the blacktop on roads and driveways to the aspirin on the shelf, from baseball bats to kitchen matches, from synthetic fabrics such as rayon to charcoal briquettes. All of these things are products of the forest.

Of nearly a thousand species of trees growing in the forests of the United States, only about one hundred are used commercially. Each of these woods is ideal for certain uses. Black walnut makes fine furniture, hickory provides tough axe handles, maple flooring stands up under generations of boots, loblolly pine can be turned into pulp and then into everything from cartons to newsprint. Until recently, the best violins were made of Norway spruce; but now a Maryland college professor thinks that Engelmann spruce may make violins with an even finer tone.

Some trees yield spices, fruits, nuts, and other forest products without being cut down. Pine trees in the Southern Forest produce resin, a thick liquid from which turpentine is made. Sections of pine bark are carefully chipped from the trunk of the tree, allowing resin to flow into pans. The tree produces resin year after year without being harmed as long as only a shallow layer of bark is removed.

Maple syrup also comes from living trees. The sap of the maple begins to flow early in the spring, and maple sugaring begins while there is still snow on the ground. The maple is tapped by drilling a hole through the bark to hold a hollow tube. The maple sap drips from the end of the tube into a bucket or plastic bag. When enough sap has been collected, it is boiled down to make a thick syrup; thirty or forty gallons of sap will make one gallon of maple syrup.

Some wood is not processed at all but simply burned for fuel. Burning firewood to keep warm is an old-fashioned way of heating that has made a comeback in the United States since the energy crisis of 1973. Before that, only about one out of seventy households had used firewood as their principal source of heat. Since that time, there has been a boom in the sale of wood stoves as people shopped around for cheaper ways to heat their homes. Seven to eight million wood stoves have been sold in the past ten years, and more and more families are sitting around by the fire on cold winter evenings.

Heating with wood is still the exception rather than the rule in most of the United States. But in some western areas, at least half the people now heat with firewood. In the Missoula Valley of Montana, the result can be seen in great clouds of smog hanging over the valley. Wood-smoke pollution has become a health problem, sending some people to hospitals. A dozen western towns and counties are now proposing laws that would limit wood burning in order to protect public health.

Industry is also using wood for fuel, although not in old-fashioned wood stoves. The paper industry burns woodchips for fuel.

About half the energy used to turn wood pulp into paper now comes from wood waste.

Christmas trees to decorate American homes are another use of forest trees. Thirty-five million trees are sold each December. Most of them are raised on special farms, of which there are about 10,000. Seedlings are ready to cut in eight to ten years—a slow crop compared with corn or potatoes, but relatively fast for the forest products industry.

The demand for wood and other forest products is greater in the United States than in any other part of the world. About half of all timber goes into lumber for building, but each person in this country also uses more than 500 pounds (227 kg) of paper each year, as well as many other by-products of the forest.

How is it possible to use so much wood and paper? The brown paper bag is a good example. Each year, supermarkets hand out 25 billion paper bags. Most of them are made in Richmond, Virginia, of wood from the loblolly pines of the Southern Forest. Nearly a thousand paper bags can be made from a single tree—which means that 25 million loblolly pines are turned into paper bags each year.

Fortunately the logging industry learned from the mistakes of the last century that the forests are *not* endless. The aim of most modern loggers is *sustained yield*—cutting only as much timber as will be replaced by new growth in any given year. It is also true, however, that some loggers see a tree in terms of the number of board feet of lumber in it. To them, a tree is something to be cut and used. Conservationists, on the other hand, see the forest in terms of watershed, scenic beauty, endangered species, and recreation. The two groups seldom see eye to eye.

Another subject on which loggers and conservationists disagree is clear-cutting—removing every tree in an area. Clear-cutting is favored by the lumber industry because it is quick and cheap. Removing timber from the forest is easier when every tree has been felled. Preparing the ground for replanting is also fairly simple, and most of the work can be done by heavy machinery.

But clear-cutting has many drawbacks. On steep slopes or in areas with fragile soil, clear-cutting is not wise because it causes erosion of the soil. It also leaves ugly scars in the forest, and when the area is replanted, all the seedlings are usually of a single species. The new growth bears little resemblance to the old forest.

Needless to say, it also disturbs wild creatures. Many birds and animals are forced out and must migrate in search of new homes. Some studies show that the shape of the clear-cut is important in its effect on wildlife. A cleared circular area may be more forbidding to animals and birds than a long, narrow ribbon of cleared land. In open fields, some forest creatures are exposed to danger from their natural enemies. They need cover and usually avoid large open spaces. On the other hand, the berries and grasses growing at the edge of a forest clearing provide food for rabbits, quail, and deer. Cutting a narrow path through a forest may result in less upheaval to its wild inhabitants. If the clear-cut follows the shape of the land, there is also a smaller risk of erosion.

Many experts think that the U.S. Forest Service has allowed too much clear-cutting in recent years. The government receives millions of dollars from the forest products industry in return for the privilege of cutting trees on federal lands. And the industry exerts a great deal of pressure on the Forest Service in its quest for more wood. This pressure is hard to resist for a number of reasons. One is the huge public demand for wood and other forest products. Each American uses more wood than a person in any other country in the world. Another reason is the size and power of the forest industry. It is so big that millions of jobs depend upon it either directly or indirectly.

Good forestry means picking the right method for the right place. Sometimes clear-cutting is the only economical way to harvest timber. But there are several other logging methods used by foresters that result in less damage to the surrounding area. They are the methods favored by many conservationists.

The *shelterwood method* removes large trees to be used as timber but leaves behind enough to provide shelter. Saplings spring up naturally and are able to grow, protected by the remaining trees from too much wind or sun.

Using the *seed tree method,* loggers remove all but a few selected trees. Those left to grow provide seed for the cleared area. After the seed trees have produced a new generation of saplings, they too are cut down.

Still another method is to cut all the trees in a small—one- or two-acre—area. (A clear-cut is apt to be closer to 100 acres [40 ha].) The surrounding forest then takes care of reseeding the cut area. This is called the *group cutting method.*

Each of these methods is less damaging to the forest than clear-cutting. But they are also slower and more expensive, partly because less of the work can be done by heavy machinery.

Today, mechanization has come to the forests and made logging much more efficient. The lumber industry uses all kinds of modern machinery to speed up the work of felling trees and getting them to the mills. The nineteenth century misery whips were long ago replaced by the power-driven chainsaw. Now trees are felled by modern machines called *feller-layers,* which cut the tree close to the ground, leaving a very short stump. A feller-layer works five times as fast as a person with a chainsaw.

For many years, lumberjacks dreamed of better ways to lift logs up and out of the forest. The spar tree, which helped hoist logs off the forest floor, was an early attempt in that direction. It has been replaced by metal poles called *tin spars.* They are mounted on motor-driven bases and are easily moved from one spot to the next.

Balloon logging came into use after World War I and is still used in some areas. Enormous helium-filled balloons are harnessed to logs and used to lift them over the treetops and then to lower them to landing sites.

A more recent development is *helilogging.* Helicopters lift and carry timber from very steep slopes and other areas that are dif-

Mechanized equipment permits
a single forester to harvest
a tree, remove its branches
and twigs, and cut it into
predetermined lengths for
transporting to the sawmill.

Trees are hauled to the
mill on heavy-duty
tractor trailers.

ficult to reach. They are able to work in rain or snow and even at night, if necessary. Only winds of over 25 knots ground them. A further advantage of helilogging is that it does less damage to remaining trees and saplings and to fragile soil than the earlier cut-and-drag methods.

Mechanical log loaders and handlers now sort, load, stack, and unload logs. Some of the diesels used to haul logs in the forest have truck beds 10 feet (3 m) wide. They are too big to use on public highways. The 500-horsepower trucks have all the latest equipment, including air-conditioned cabs and electronic weighing devices.

All of the modern machinery now used in the forests is linked by intercom and shortwave radio. And when the logs finally reach the sawmill, they are turned into forest products with the help of modern technology. If the aim of modern loggers is sustained yield, the aim of the mill operators is full utilization—making the best possible use of every tree.

Less than a century ago, sawmills wasted most of every tree they handled. Only about one-third wound up as usable lumber. The rest was either burned or left to decay. Today, nearly every scrap is used. Stronger metals have helped cut down on waste. Thinner saw blades make less sawdust, both in the woods and at the mills.

When timber arrives at the mill, a high-speed stripping machine removes the outer bark from the trunk. This bark is marketed as mulch or fuel. Mulch is a covering used around plantings to help keep the soil moist. Next, the rounded side slabs of the log are reduced to small bits by a chipping machine. The chips go to a pulp mill, where they are used to make paper or are burned as fuel. Heavy beams are cut from the knotty center of the log, leaving the choicest wood to be sawed into boards or planks.

Modern sawmills are multimillion-dollar plants. They are safe, fast, and well-lighted. The newest mills are largely run by computers. Much of the work of the old-time head sawyer is now done by photoelectric scanners and computers. The best use of each log is determined by photosensors. The computer then chooses

The modern sawmill uses computers and photoelectric scanners to sort and process the logs.

from among several thousand different patterns the one that is best for handling that particular log. Once it has been cut, lumber is carted off by conveyor belt and mechanically sorted according to size and quality.

New ways of using wood have also helped reduce waste. *Plywood* is one fairly recent development—a "modern" invention that actually dates from the time of the Egyptian pharaohs; the same technique was finally tried in this country in 1865.

In order to make plywood, a tree is peeled: a sharp blade the length of the log peels off a very thin continuous sheet of wood, in much the same way an apple might be peeled. The thin sheets, or *veneers,* are made into a sandwich of about five layers, with each sheet of veneer at right angles to those above and below it. The layers are glued and then pressed together. The plywood made in this way is extremely light and strong. It can be made of wood that is not as free of flaws as that used for solid planks. A round core of wood is all that remains after a tree has been peeled. Even the core is not wasted; it makes an excellent fence post.

Plywood makes it possible to use smaller trees than in the past. Instead of cutting boards and beams from massive forest monarchs, trees as small as fifteen inches in diameter can be peeled and used to make plywood. Most of these smaller trees come from the Southern Forest. As a result of the demand for plywood, the center of the lumber industry has shifted once again—this time from the Northwest to the South.

One of the major uses of wood is for making paper. One mill in Wauna, Oregon, turns out enough paper each day to form a ribbon 10 feet (3 m) wide and 4,320 miles (6,955 km) long— enough to stretch from New York City to Los Angeles and back to Louisville, Kentucky. Wauna is located on the Columbia River, from which the mill draws 40 million gallons (150 million l) of water each day. Every drop of it has to be treated to remove the chemicals used in paper-making before it can be returned to the river. Even the air is "scrubbed" in a not entirely successful attempt to rid it of the rotten-egg smell caused by hydrogen sulphide, one of the chemicals used in making paper.

One way to cut down on the demand for pulpwood is by *recycling* paper—using it more than once. Many communities now have recycling centers where used newspapers and magazines are collected. Recycled paper can be used for all newsprint—and if all newsprint were made in this way, the savings would be enormous. According to one estimate, a single edition of a large Sunday paper uses 252 acres (102 ha) of forest trees. At the moment, only small amounts of paper are being recycled. But as the demand for wood products increases, more recycled paper will certainly be used.

There is also a search going on for wood substitutes. In Africa, foresters have found a fast-growing plant that could be used instead of pulpwood for making paper. It is called kenaf, and it grows 15 feet (5 m) in a single season. When planted in rows, like corn, it produces five times as much fiber as pulpwood trees. Kenaf can be ground up and used in place of wood in papermaking. It is one of a number of possible substitutes that are being studied.

Nearly all forests still depend upon natural reseeding. But a small number are seeded or replanted by people. This is called tree farming because the trees are raised in much the same way that farmers grow oats or beans. The first step in replanting a logged area is getting rid of the slash, which is reduced to chips and mulched into the ground by heavy tractors or harrows. If the area is flat enough, tree-planting machines are sometimes used next. The largest of these machines is able to handle 10,000 tiny seedlings a day—enough to reforest 10 or 15 acres (4 or 6 ha).

Above: *the pulping process is one of the most important steps in turning trees into paper.* Below: *the paper is wound on large rolls, sometimes over 20 feet (6 m) wide.*

Tree farmers usually plant just one kind of tree, so, of course, they want to use seedlings that are fast-growing and disease-resistant. As a result, plant breeding has become an important job for the experts.

Foresters search the woods for hardwood trees that are particularly healthy, strong, and tall. They cut branches from these wild trees and then graft them to saplings in a nursery bed. When the grafted saplings produce seed, it is gathered and sown in another bed, where it is carefully tended

Pollinating by hand is another method of plant breeding. Bags are placed over a plant's female flowers to keep them from being pollinated by the wind. Pollen is then removed from a second plant, which may have been chosen for a different set of traits. For example, one plant might be especially straight, and the other might be fast-growing. By crossbreeding two selected plants, foresters have been able to produce better strains of trees.

Loblolly pine is one tree that has been improved by plant breeding. The amount of timber produced by an acre of loblolly pine has tripled in the last twenty years. Other coniferous trees that would take from 60 to 100 years to grow to full size in a natural forest are now ready to be cut after about 35 years. The time between planting and harvesting has been cut in half.

These are just a few of the ways used by the experts to improve trees. Perhaps the most futuristic method is *cloning*—producing exact copies of good tree stock. Researchers are trying to produce such clones by culturing plant tissue in the laboratory. Someday, there may be whole forests of nearly identical trees as a result of their work.

It is estimated that the use of wood and forest products in the United States, already the greatest in the world, may double in the next few decades. This country has large reserves of wood—about 12 percent of the world's supply. Still, the danger remains that without careful planning, we may use up the forests faster than they can grow back. This has already happened in many parts of the world.

AFTERWORD

THE WORLDWIDE FOREST

Forests not only supply many of today's needs, they also affect tomorrow's world. One important way in which they affect the future, as well as the present, is by serving as a *genetic bank*. The wilderness safeguards many species of plants as well as animals. When domestic crops are stricken and perhaps wiped out by disease or other disasters, scientists can go back to the wilderness to find older strains of the same plant. If all domestic wheat were to die in a single season, for example, a very similar grain could probably be produced by crossbreeding wild varieties.

The forests, and especially the tropical rain forests, contain an enormous variety of useful plants. Many of them have been known for centuries, but others are being found each year. Some of the drugs from the forest that were used by early people are still in use today. Both the ancient Greeks and the American Indians knew that bark from the willow tree relieves pain. Today, it is called "aspirin"—one of the most widely used drugs. Nearly 45 percent of all the drugs prescribed by doctors are made of ingredients from the rain forest. Other early natural remedies may have been forgotten, but they still exist in the forest and are waiting to be rediscovered.

World forests also affect the Earth's climate and its supply of fresh water. Dense forests actually help make their own climate. The rain forests of the tropics cannot grow except in very wet areas. But it is equally true that if they were destroyed, the areas now covered by these forests would become much drier.

In South America's Amazon Basin lies the world's largest tropical rain forest. It is ten times as big as Texas. Half of the rain that falls in this huge area is created by the forest itself. As a result of this heavy rain, the area is a watery wilderness. Nearly two-thirds of all the fresh water in the world is held by the Amazon Basin. If the Amazon rain forest no longer existed, the whole area might become a desert. The world's cycle of fresh water would change and even the Earth's climate would be affected.

One result might be a build-up of carbon dioxide (CO_2) in the earth's atmosphere. CO_2 is one of the gases that affects world climate. It is absorbed and stored by the trees of the forest. When forests are cleared and the wood in their trees burns or decays, the CO_2 is returned to the atmosphere.

During the past few decades, the amount of CO_2 in the atmosphere has increased sharply. The build-up has probably been caused mainly by gases released by burning coal and oil. But a second reason for the increase is the loss of forest trees that absorb CO_2. If too much CO_2 accumulated in the atmosphere (and no one knows for sure just how much is "too much"), this is what scientists think might happen: the Earth would gradually become warmer; as polar ice caps melted, the level of the oceans would rise; the land mass of the earth would become smaller. The result would be less land and fewer forests to be shared by ever-increasing numbers of people.

Of the world's four natural resources—water, fossil fuels, minerals, and forests—only water and forests are renewable. Given half a chance, trees will struggle to grow, even on land that has been cleared. But forests have already shrunk alarmingly, and human demands continue to grow. They will become even more pressing as world population increases. There will be a greater need for fuel and for all the other products of the forest. More people will use them for recreation, and the beauty of wild scenic areas will become rarer and more precious. Wildlife will be in even greater need of the protection the forest gives.

It may not be possible to satisfy all of these competing demands. Long-term planning and research will be required in order to balance them out and maintain healthy forests. Above all, an understanding of the nature of forests and of the many roles they play will be needed if forests are to continue to serve and inspire "the people unborn as well as the people now alive."

GLOSSARY

arson—malicious burning of any property.

bulls—name used by lumberjacks for oxen.

bull-whacker—person who drives a bull team.

chute—wooden trough used as a slide to carry logs downhill.

clear-cutting—cutting down all the trees in a large area.

cloning—creating identical copies.

conifers—cone-bearing trees, usually evergreen, such as pine, fir, and spruce.

crown fire—a fire that rises from the base of a tree, then spreads from treetop to treetop.

deciduous—trees, such as oak, that shed their leaves annually.

Dolbeer donkey—crude steam engine used in early logging.

feller-layer—machine used to cut down trees.

flume—wooden trough filled with water used to carry logs downhill.

genetic bank—in forestry, an area containing wild species that may be used to develop new domestic strains.

greaser—person who greased the skid road, making it easier to "skid" logs out of the woods.

group cutting method—cutting down all the trees in a small area.

handcar—small railroad car, propelled by hand, used to transport people.

hardwood—trees yielding hard, compact wood, such as oak, cherry, and maple.

helilogging—use of helicopters to lift logs out of the forest.

high climber—person who climbs and tops tall trees.

hoot-owl logging—early morning logging, while the air is moist.

Hot Shot crews—highly trained firefighters of the U.S. Forest Service.

hot spot—place where fire is burning most vigorously.

infrared sensor—device used to locate fires.

log boom—floating raft of logs.

logged-over—cleared of trees by logging.

lumberjack—person who works at logging.

misery whips—large crosscut saws used in early logging.

mulch—woodchips, leaves, or other material that keep the soil moist.

multiple use—use of an area for several different purposes.

peavey—a short pole with a sharply pointed end.

plywood—boards made by pressing and gluing thin sheets of wood together.

pole train—train carrying logs on flatbed cars.

pulpwood—trees from which wood pulp is made.

recycle—to use something over again.

seed tree method—leaving some trees for natural reseeding in a logged area.

shelterwood method—leaving enough trees in a logged area to provide shelter for saplings.

skid road—road made by felling saplings and using their trunks as a base.

slash—leaves, branches, twigs, and sawdust left after logging or at a mill.

smoke jumpers—firefighters who parachute into remote areas.

spar tree—tall trunk left standing, used in lifting logs.

sustained yield—cutting only as much timber as will be replaced by annual growth.

tin spar—a tall, metal pole on a wheeled base, used in lifting logs.

topping—cutting off the top of a standing tree.

veneer—thin sheet of wood used in making plywood.

watershed—area serving as a natural water reserve.

wigwam burner—structure shaped like a teepee, used at sawmills to burn slash.

wood pulp—treated wood used in making paper.

FURTHER READING

The International Book of the Forest. New York: Simon & Schuster, 1981.

Ketchum, Richard M. *The Secret Life of the Forest.* New York: American Heritage, 1970.

Page, Jack. *Forest.* Alexandria, VA: Time-Life Books, 1983.

INDEX

Photographs indicated by *italic* numbers.

Acid rain, 34–35
Adirondack Mountains, N.Y., 34
Amazon Basin, 56
American chestnut, 25
American Indians, 4, 25, 29, 31, 35
Atlantic Plain, 28

Bald cypress, 28
Bark beetle, 31
Beech, 27
Black walnut, 43
Boise National Forest, Idaho, *36*
Bristlecone pine, 19, 23

Camels Hump, Vermont, 35
Carbon dioxide, 56
Central Forest, 19, *21*, 27
Cohutta Wilderness Area, Georgia, 41
Commercial forest area, 13–14
Conifers, 22
Conservation of forest resources, 2, 13, 45, 46–47, 54–57
Controlled burns, *40*, 42
Cottonwood, 27
Crown fire, 35, *36*, 37, 41–42

Deciduous trees, 27
Demand for lumber and forest products, 4, 43, 44, 46, 53, 55–56, 57
Depletion of forest resources, 2, 10–11, 13, 30–42, 54, 56–57
Douglas fir, 22, 23, 37, 38
Dutch elm disease, 31

Ecosystem, forest, 12, 30–31, 42
Elm, 27, 31
Engelmann spruce, 23, 43
Environmental effects of forested areas, 10–11, 12, 17–18, 28, 30–31, 34–35, 37–38, 44, 46, 49, 56–57
Erosion, 10–11, 28, 46, 49

Fire fighting/prevention, 38, *39*, *40*, 41–42
Firewood, 44–45
Florida Everglades, 28
Forest fires, 2, 10, 35–42
Forest products, 1, 6, 43–54, 55–57
Forest Service, 13, 15, 38–41, 46
Full utilization concept, 49

Gales Creek Canyon, Oregon, 37
Genetic bank, 55–56
Giant sequoia, 19, 22